JAWEED YAMANI

A VISIONARY LEADER

WRITER
VIKRAM KULKARNI

FOREWORD

SOME ENTREPRENEURS BREAK RECORDS; OTHERS BREAK BARRIERS. JAWEED YAMAANI, RECOGNIZED AS ONE OF THE 40 UNDER 40 ENTREPRENEURS OF THE YEAR IN 2024, IS A LEADER WHO HAS DONE BOTH. BY THE AGE OF 25, HE HAD ALREADY ESTABLISHED SEVEN GROUNDBREAKING VENTURES, EACH ADDRESSING CRITICAL GAPS IN EMPLOYMENT, HEALTHCARE, MARKETING, AND MORE. THIS BOOK IS A TESTAMENT TO HIS JOURNEY, WHICH BEGAN WHEN HE WAS JUST 21, AND HIS UNWAVERING COMMITMENT TO EMPOWERING PEOPLE AND RESHAPING INDUSTRIES. PERSONAL REFLECTIONS IN THE FOREWORD, WE REFLECT ON JAWEED'S PERSONAL QUALITIES THAT HAVE DRIVEN HIS SUCCESS. WE DELVE INTO HIS EARLY MOTIVATIONS, HIS RESILIENCE, AND THE VALUES THAT HAVE GUIDED HIM THROUGHOUT HIS JOURNEY.

CHAPTER 1: JAWEED'S EARLY JOURNEY

COLLEGE LIFE OF JAWEED YAMANI

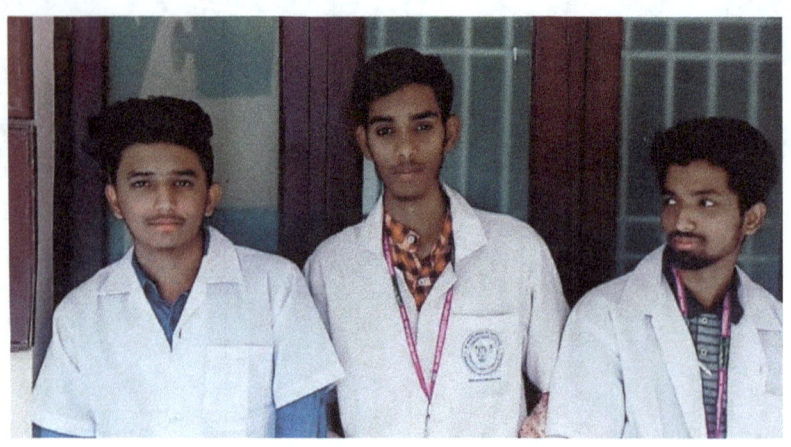

AT THE INITIAL STAGE OF JAWEED YAMANI'S JOURNEY, HE WAS A BTECH MECHANICAL ENGINEERING DROPOUT. FINANCIAL STRUGGLES FORCED HIM TO LEAVE HIS STUDIES, AND HE STARTED SELLING GOGGLES AT CHARMINAR EARLY IN THE MORNING FROM 7 AM TO 10 AM. FROM THIS, HE EARNED ABOUT ₹100 PER DAY.

LATER, JAWEED YAMANI WORKED AS A SALESMAN AT YS STORE, A CLOTHING SHOP IN KHILWATH NEAR CHARMINAR, WHERE HIS MONTHLY SALARY WAS ₹3,500. HE CONTINUED JUGGLING THESE ROLES FOR TWO YEARS.

WHEN THE COVID-19 LOCKDOWN HIT, JAWEED YAMANI TOOK UP A JOB AS A DELIVERY BOY AT AMAZON. HE WORKED THERE FOR SIX MONTHS.

"RARE PICTURES OF JAWEED DURING HIS TIME AS A DELIVERY BOY."

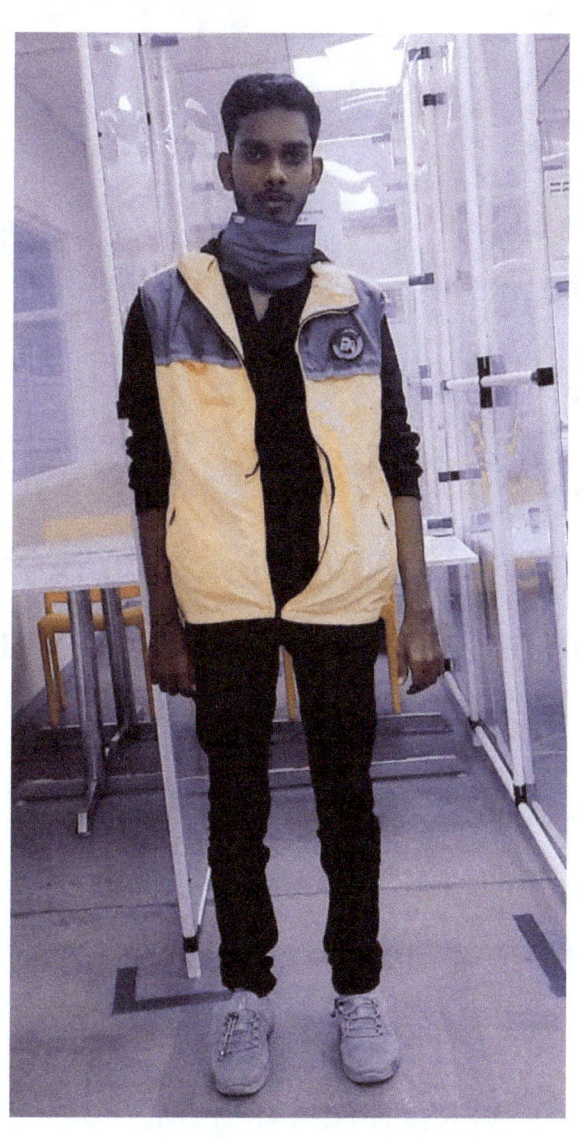

DURING THIS TIME, ONE OF JAWEED YAMANI'S SUPERVISORS LEFT, AND THAT'S WHEN HIS LIFE TOOK A PIVOTAL TURN. HIS ROLE MODEL, MENTOR, AND SOURCE OF INSPIRATION, ASIF RUBSAMJANI, WHO WAS HIS MANAGER AT AMAZON, GAVE HIM AN OPPORTUNITY TO BECOME A STATION SUPERVISOR. THIS CHANCE CHANGED EVERYTHING FOR HIM.

KEY INFLUENCES

- THE PIVOTAL ROLE OF ASIF RUBSAMJANI IN MY LIFE

- THE MENTORSHIP AND LESSONS LEARNED FROM HIM

- THE TRANSITION FROM FEAR OF LOSING A JOB TO GAINING CONFIDENCE

LIFE AS A SUPERVISOR

WHILE WORKING AS A SUPERVISOR FOR SEVEN MONTHS, JAWEED YAMANI OFTEN FEARED LOSING THE JOB AND WORRIED ABOUT HOW HE'D MANAGE TO FIND ANOTHER ONE. THE THOUGHT OF RETURNING TO A DELIVERY BOY ROLE CONSTANTLY HAUNTED HIM. HOWEVER, ASIF GUIDANCE'S AND ENCOURAGEMENT HELPED HIM NAVIGATE THESE FEARS.

ASIF RUBSAMJANI BELIEVED IN JAWEED YAMANI AND TAUGHT HIM INVALUABLE LESSONS. AFTER SEVEN MONTHS, BOTH OF THEM MOVED TO ANOTHER COMPANY TOGETHER, WHERE JAWEED CONTINUED TO LEARN UNDER ASIF'S MENTORSHIP FOR A YEAR.

CONTINUING THE JOURNEY

JAWEED CREDITS WHO HE IS TODAY TO ASIF RUBSAMJANI, WHO GAVE HIM THE CHANCE TO TRANSFORM HIS LIFE FROM BEING A DELIVERY BOY TO AN ENTREPRENEUR. AFTER THAT YEAR, ASIF AND JAWEED JOINED SEPARATE COMPANIES, BUT THEIR BOND REMAINED STRONG. TO THIS DAY, ASIF IS JUST A PHONE CALL AWAY WHENEVER JAWEED NEEDS ADVICE OR SUPPORT

FACING CHALLENGES

IN THE FOLLOWING YEARS, JAWEED YAMANI WORKED WITH ONE OR TWO OTHER COMPANIES BUT FACED SIGNIFICANT CHALLENGES, SUCH AS NOT RECEIVING HIS SALARY ON TIME. DESPITE THESE HURDLES, HE PERSEVERED, DRAWING STRENGTH FROM THE LESSONS HE HAD LEARNED UNDER ASIF RUBSAMJANI. IT WAS DURING THESE TOUGH TIMES THAT JAWEED REALIZED HOW CHALLENGING IT IS FOR PEOPLE TO FIND JOBS. THIS REALIZATION FUELED HIS AMBITION TO CREATE A PLATFORM WHERE INDIVIDUALS CAN ACCESS JOB OPPORTUNITIES WITHOUT ANY COST AND CONNECT WITH GOOD COMPANIES. HIS AIM IS SIMPLE: TO MAKE JOB SEARCHES EASIER AND FREE FOR EVERYONE.

SUPPORT FROM AMER PASHA

ONE MORE PERSON WHO PLAYED A CRUCIAL ROLE IN MY JOURNEY IS AMER PASHA. WE WORKED TOGETHER AT AMAZON, WHERE HE WAS PART OF MY TEAM. OVER THE PAST FIVE YEARS, AMER HAS BECOME A CLOSE FRIEND,

"THEY STILL MEET REGULARLY TO SHARE CHAI AND HAVE CONVERSATIONS. AMER, A TALENTED BACKEND AND FRONTEND DEVELOPER, HELPED JAWEED BUILD HIS WEBSITE. HE WORKED TIRELESSLY ON BOTH THE BACKEND AND FRONTEND ASPECTS OF THE PLATFORM, ENSURING IT FUNCTIONED SEAMLESSLY AND MET THE NEEDS OF USERS."

"HIS TECHNICAL EXPERTISE AND UNWAVERING SUPPORT HAVE BEEN INSTRUMENTAL IN BRINGING JAWEED'S VISION TO LIFE. AMER'S CONTRIBUTION

AMER'S CONTRIBUTION DIDN'T STOP AT JUST DEVELOPING THE WEBSITE. HE ALSO PROVIDED VALUABLE INSIGHTS AND SUGGESTIONS TO ENHANCE THE PLATFORM'S USER EXPERIENCE. HIS DEDICATION AND FRIENDSHIP HAVE BEEN A SOURCE OF STRENGTH AND MOTIVATION FOR JAWEED THROUGHOUT THIS JOURNEY."

CURRENT MISSION

"TODAY, JAWEED'S JOURNEY FROM A DELIVERY BOY TO AN ENTREPRENEUR IS A TESTAMENT TO THE POWER OF PERSEVERANCE, MENTORSHIP, AND STRONG FRIENDSHIPS. HIS MISSION IS TO CREATE OPPORTUNITIES AND MAKE THE JOB MARKET ACCESSIBLE TO ALL, ENSURING THAT NO ONE HAS TO FACE THE STRUGGLES HE ONCE DID."

CHAPTER 2: THE SPARK OF AN IDEA

AT 21, JAWEED YAMAANI STOOD AT A CROSSROADS, ARMED WITH LITTLE MORE THAN AMBITION AND A DEEP UNDERSTANDING OF THE STRUGGLES FACED BY EVERYDAY PEOPLE. GROWING UP, HE SAW TALENTED INDIVIDUALS STRUGGLE

TO FIND JOBS, SMALL BUSINESSES FALTER DUE TO LACK OF RESOURCES, AND ENTIRE COMMUNITIES DEPRIVED OF BASIC HEALTHCARE. THESE CHALLENGES INSPIRED HIM TO ACT.

THE EARLY YEARS

JAWEED'S UPBRINGING IN A TIGHT-KNIT COMMUNITY GAVE HIM A UNIQUE PERSPECTIVE ON THE IMPORTANCE OF OPPORTUNITY. HE WITNESSED FIRSTHAND THE STRUGGLES AND TRIUMPHS OF THOSE AROUND HIM, FOSTERING A DEEP SENSE OF EMPATHY AND A DESIRE TO MAKE A DIFFERENCE.

THE BIRTH OF A SOLUTION

WHAT STARTED AS A SMALL RECRUITMENT INITIATIVE SOON EXPANDED INTO A MULTI-INDUSTRY POWERHOUSE. JAWEED'S ABILITY TO ENVISION SOLUTIONS AND EXECUTE THEM WITH PRECISION BECAME HIS HALLMARK.

CHAPTER 3: THE 40 UNDER 40 MILESTONE

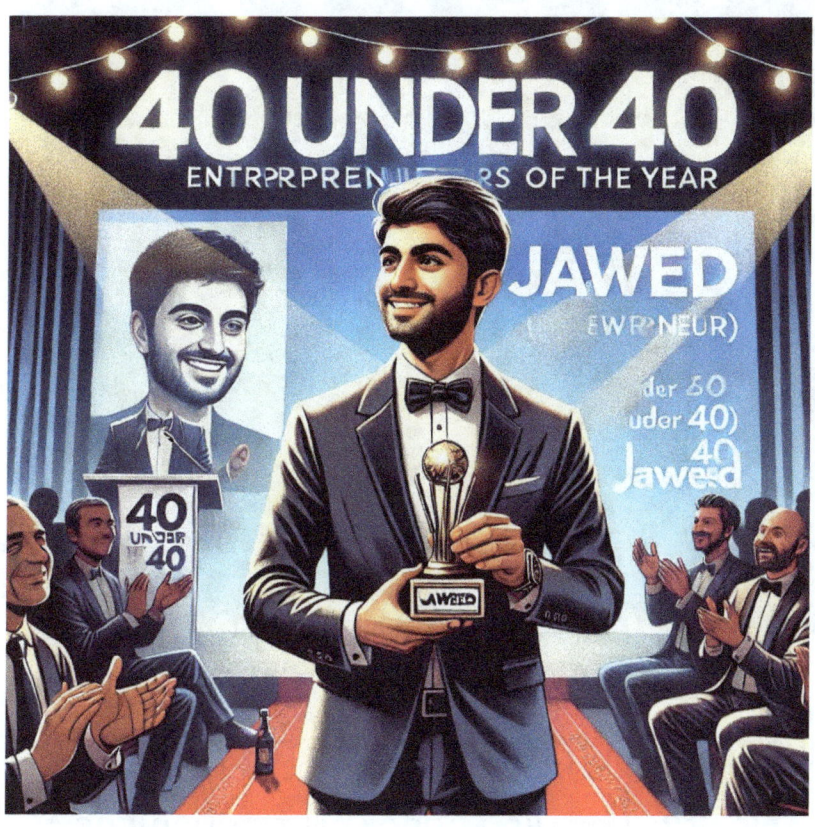

BY 2024, JAWEED'S ACHIEVEMENTS HAD EARNED HIM A PLACE ON THE PRESTIGIOUS 40 UNDER 40 ENTREPRENEURS OF THE YEAR LIST. THIS RECOGNITION WAS A CELEBRATION OF HIS

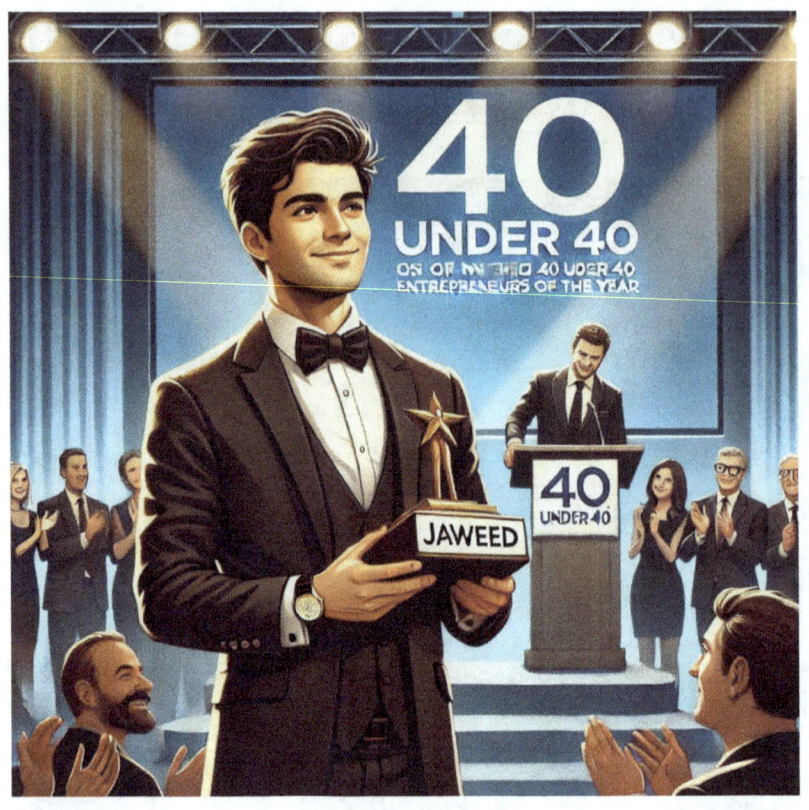

THE IMPACT JAWEED'S RECOGNITION WASN'T JUST A PERSONAL MILESTONE; IT WAS A VALIDATION OF HIS APPROACH TO BUSINESS AND LEADERSHIP. HIS STORY INSPIRED COUNTLESS YOUNG ENTREPRENEURS TO PURSUE THEIR DREAMS, PROVING THAT AGE IS NO BARRIER TO SUCCESS WHEN DRIVEN BY PASSION AND PURPOSE.

CHAPTER 4: NETZENHR – REVOLUTIONIZING HUMAN RESOURCES

JAWEED'S FIRST VENTURE, NETZENHR, REDEFINED HOW COMPANIES APPROACHED WORKFORCE MANAGEMENT. AT ITS CORE, NETZENHR WAS BUILT ON JAWEED'S BELIEF THAT BUSINESSES SUCCEED WHEN THEY PRIORITIZE THEIR PEOPLE. BY DEVELOPING TOOLS THAT STREAMLINED RECRUITMENT, ONBOARDING, AND EMPLOYEE RETENTION, JAWEED PROVIDED COMPANIES WITH THE MEANS TO BUILD STRONGER, HAPPIER TEAMS.

INNOVATIVE SOLUTIONS

NETZENHR INTRODUCED A SUITE OF INNOVATIVE TOOLS DESIGNED TO SIMPLIFY HR PROCESSES. FROM AI-DRIVEN RECRUITMENT ALGORITHMS TO COMPREHENSIVE EMPLOYEE WELLNESS PROGRAMS, JAWEED'S SOLUTIONS WERE TAILORED TO MEET THE EVOLVING NEEDS OF MODERN BUSINESSES.

BUILDING A STRONG WORKFORCE

THROUGH NETZENHR, JAWEED EMPHASIZED THE IMPORTANCE OF NURTURING TALENT AND FOSTERING A POSITIVE WORK ENVIRONMENT. HIS APPROACH HELPED COMPANIES ATTRACT AND RETAIN TOP TALENT, ULTIMATELY DRIVING BUSINESS SUCCESS AND EMPLOYEE SATISFACTION.

CHAPTER 5: DIGNITY JOBS – A MISSION TO RESTORE HOPE

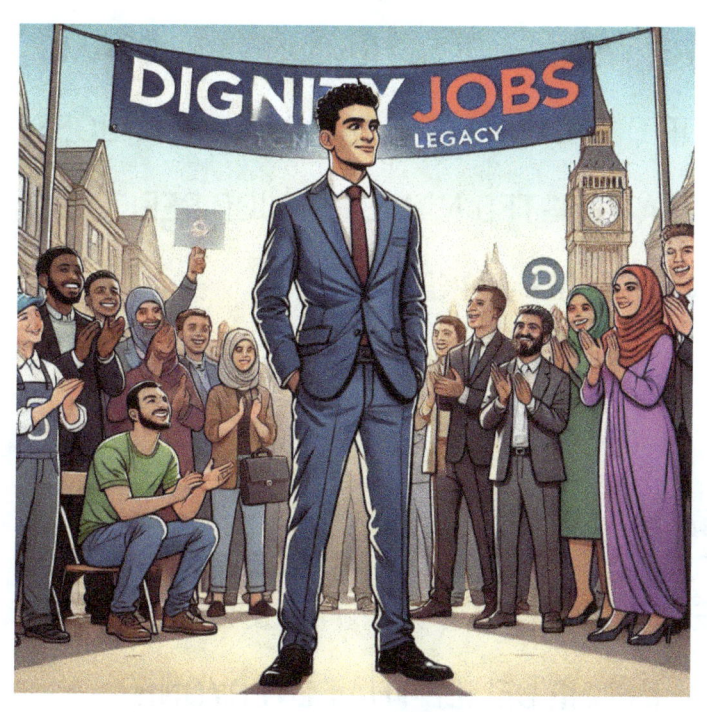

DIGNITY JOBS IS THE CORNERSTONE OF JAWEED'S LEGACY. LAUNCHED TO TACKLE UNEMPLOYMENT, THIS PLATFORM OFFERED **FREE JOB OPPORTUNITIES TO OVER 25,000** CANDIDATES, TRANSFORMING LIVES ACROSS THE NATION JAWEED BELIEVED THAT EMPLOYMENT WAS MORE THAN JUST A PAYCHECK—IT WAS A SOURCE OF DIGNITY AND PRIDE.

THROUGH WORKSHOPS, TRAINING PROGRAMS, AND ONE-ON-ONE MENTORSHIP, DIGNITY JOBS BECAME A TRUSTED NAME FOR JOB SEEKERS AND EMPLOYERS ALIKE.

EMPOWERING INDIVIDUALS

JAWEED'S VISION FOR DIGNITY JOBS WAS ROOTED IN THE BELIEF THAT EVERYONE DESERVES A CHANCE TO SUCCEED. THE PLATFORM'S COMPREHENSIVE SUPPORT SYSTEM EMPOWERED INDIVIDUALS TO BUILD FULFILLING CAREERS AND ACHIEVE FINANCIAL INDEPENDENCE.

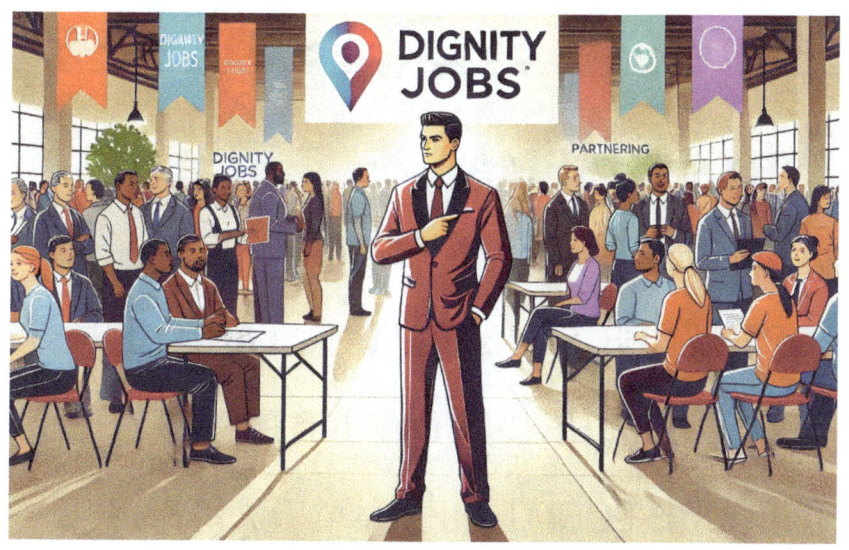

CREATING OPPORTUNITIES

DIGNITY JOBS PARTNERED WITH VARIOUS ORGANIZATIONS TO CREATE A DIVERSE RANGE OF JOB OPPORTUNITIES. FROM ENTRY-LEVEL POSITIONS TO SKILLED TRADES, THE PLATFORM CATERED TO A WIDE SPECTRUM OF JOB SEEKERS, HELPING THEM FIND MEANINGFUL WORK.

PERSONAL SUCCESS STORIES

1. **RIYA SHARMA**,

A FRESH GRADUATE WITH LIMITED WORK EXPERIENCE, STRUGGLED TO LAND HER FIRST JOB. SHE DISCOVERED DIGNITY JOBS THROUGH SOCIAL MEDIA AND ATTENDED ONE OF THEIR JOB FAIRS. WITH THE GUIDANCE PROVIDED DURING THE EVENT AND TAILORED RESUME ADVICE, SHE SECURED HER FIRST ROLE AS A MARKETING ASSOCIATE AT A REPUTABLE FIRM. TODAY, RIYA IS THRIVING IN HER CAREER AND ATTRIBUTES HER BREAKTHROUGH TO THE PLATFORM'S COMMITMENT TO EMPOWERING JOB SEEKERS.

2. VIKRAM PATEL,

AFTER LOSING HIS JOB DURING AN ECONOMIC DOWNTURN, A SKILLED ELECTRICIAN, WAS UNCERTAIN ABOUT HIS FUTURE. **DIGNITY JOBS** CONNECTED HIM WITH A GROWING CONSTRUCTION COMPANY LOOKING FOR TALENTED TRADESPEOPLE. THROUGH THEIR NETWORK, VIKRAM NOT ONLY FOUND A JOB BUT ALSO GAINED ACCESS TO TRAINING SESSIONS THAT HELPED HIM ENHANCE HIS SKILLS. NOW, HE'S A LEAD SUPERVISOR AND MENTORS OTHERS ENTERING THE TRADE.

3. NEHA

AFTER YEARS OF BEING A HOMEMAKER, DECIDED TO RE-ENTER THE WORKFORCE BUT WAS UNSURE OF WHERE TO BEGIN. THROUGH **DIGNITY JOBS**, SHE DISCOVERED REMOTE WORKING OPPORTUNITIES WITH FLEXIBLE HOURS. SHE WAS HIRED AS A CUSTOMER SUPPORT EXECUTIVE FOR A GLOBAL E-COMMERCE FIRM. TODAY, NEHA BALANCES HER FAMILY AND CAREER EFFORTLESSLY AND IS AN INSPIRATION TO OTHERS IN HER COMMUNITY.

4.ISHAQ

A VISUALLY IMPAIRED SOFTWARE DEVELOPER, FACED CONSTANT REJECTIONS DESPITE HIS QUALIFICATIONS. DIGNITY JOBS PARTNERED WITH AN INCLUSIVE TECH STARTUP AND CONNECTED ARJUN WITH THEIR HIRING TEAM. HIS TECHNICAL EXPERTISE AND DETERMINATION EARNED HIM A ROLE AS A BACKEND DEVELOPER. ARJUN NOW ADVOCATES FOR INCLUSIVITY IN THE WORKPLACE, AND HIS STORY HAS INSPIRED MANY COMPANIES TO EMBRACE DIVERSE HIRING PRACTICES.

5. MUSTAFA

Through **Dignity Jobs' Affiliate Services,** Mustafa discovered earning opportunities in the gig economy. She started as a freelance content writer and, with consistent support from the platform, grew her network of clients. Today, Meera runs her own digital content agency, employing others who are just starting their careers.

6. ALI KHAN,

A COLLEGE DROPOUT, WAS DISHEARTENED ABOUT HIS PROSPECTS. THROUGH DIGNITY JOBS, HE FOUND A MENTORSHIP PROGRAM AND AN APPRENTICESHIP IN A TECH FIRM. ALI EXCELLED IN HIS ROLE AND WAS EVENTUALLY HIRED FULL-TIME AS A SOFTWARE DEVELOPER. TODAY, HE MENTORS OTHERS FACING SIMILAR CHALLENGES, GIVING BACK TO THE PLATFORM THAT GAVE HIM HOPE.

7. RAMESH YADAV

IN A SMALL VILLAGE, , A HIGH SCHOOL GRADUATE, DREAMED OF MOVING TO THE CITY FOR BETTER OPPORTUNITIES. WITH LIMITED RESOURCES, HE CONNECTED WITH **DIGNITY JOBS,** WHICH INTRODUCED HIM TO AN ENTRY-LEVEL ROLE IN LOGISTICS. NOW, RAMESH WORKS AS A WAREHOUSE MANAGER, SUPPORTING HIS FAMILY AND INSPIRING OTHERS IN HIS COMMUNITY TO PURSUE THEIR DREAMS.

THESE SUCCESS STORIES DEMONSTRATE THE TRANSFORMATIVE POWER OF DIGNITY JOBS, WHICH NOT ONLY PROVIDES OPPORTUNITIES BUT ALSO INSTILLS HOPE AND EMPOWERS INDIVIDUALS TO OVERCOME THEIR CHALLENGES. THEIR IMPACT CONTINUES TO GROW AS THEY BRIDGE GAPS BETWEEN JOB SEEKERS AND EMPLOYERS, CREATING A BETTER FUTURE FOR ALL.

IMPACT OF PARTNERSHIPS

THESE COLLABORATIONS HAVE NOT ONLY EXPANDED DIGNITY JOBS' REACH BUT ALSO STRENGTHENED ITS ABILITY TO CATER TO DIVERSE JOB SEEKERS. BY ALIGNING WITH ORGANIZATIONS THAT SHARE A COMMON GOAL, DIGNITY JOBS CONTINUES TO CREATE AN ECOSYSTEM WHERE OPPORTUNITIES ARE ACCESSIBLE TO ALL, PAVING THE WAY FOR A MORE INCLUSIVE WORKFORCE.

CHAPTER 6: DIGNITY EARNING SERVICES – CREATING PATHWAYS TO PROSPERITY

During his early days, Jaweed realized that financial independence was a universal aspiration, and Dignity Earning Services was born to meet this need. The platform provided individuals with freelance, remote, and gig-based work opportunities, especially during uncertain economic times. Jaweed's ability to adapt quickly to changing

MARKETS MADE THIS VENTURE A LIFELINE FOR THOUSANDS.

ADAPTING TO CHANGE

DIGNITY EARNING SERVICES RESPONDED TO THE SHIFTING ECONOMIC LANDSCAPE BY OFFERING FLEXIBLE WORK OPTIONS. THIS ADAPTABILITY ALLOWED INDIVIDUALS TO NAVIGATE ECONOMIC UNCERTAINTIES AND MAINTAIN FINANCIAL STABILITY.

SUPPORTING FREELANCERS

THE PLATFORM'S RESOURCES AND SUPPORT FOR FREELANCERS HELPED THEM THRIVE IN A COMPETITIVE MARKET. JAWEED'S COMMITMENT TO PROVIDING VALUABLE OPPORTUNITIES ENSURED THAT USERS COULD ACHIEVE THEIR FINANCIAL GOALS AND BUILD SUCCESSFUL CAREERS.

JOB CREATION:

ENABLED OVER **10,000** INDIVIDUALS TO FIND SUSTAINABLE REMOTE WORK. INCOME GENERATION: BOOSTED HOUSEHOLD INCOMES BY FACILITATING ACCESS TO HIGH-PAYING FREELANCE OPPORTUNITIES.

COMMUNITY DEVELOPMENT:

SUPPORTED SKILL-BUILDING INITIATIVES, FOSTERING ECONOMIC GROWTH IN UNDERREPRESENTED AREAS.

PROVIDE DATA AND METRICS THAT SHOWCASE THE PLATFORM'S ROLE IN EMPOWERING ECONOMIC INDEPENDENCE AND REDUCING UNEMPLOYMENT.

FUTURE PLANS

GLOBAL EXPANSION:

PLANS TO EXTEND SERVICES TO UNDERSERVED REGIONS, CREATING A WORLDWIDE NETWORK OF REMOTE WORKERS.

SKILL DEVELOPMENT PROGRAMS:

LAUNCHING FREE OR AFFORDABLE COURSES TO HELP USERS UPGRADE THEIR SKILLS AND STAY COMPETITIVE.

PARTNERSHIPS:

COLLABORATING WITH MORE BUSINESSES AND ORGANIZATIONS TO OFFER DIVERSE OPPORTUNITIES.

COMMUNITY BUILDING

CREATING FORUMS AND EVENTS TO ENHANCE COLLABORATION AND LEARNING AMONG FREELANCERS.

CHAPTER 7 : DIGNITY ARKETING SERVICES GIVING BRANDS A VOICE

N AN ERA WHERE ATTENTION IS CURRENCY, JAWEED CREATED DIGNITY MARKETING SERVICES TO HELP BRANDS CRAFT COMPELLING NARRATIVES. THE AGENCY BLENDED CREATIVE STORYTELLING WITH DATA-DRIVEN STRATEGIES, ALLOWING BUSINESSES TO CONNECT DEEPLY WITH THEIR AUDIENCES. JAWEED'S PERSONAL INVOLVEMENT IN UNDERSTANDING CONSUMER BEHAVIOR SET THIS VENTURE APART, MAKING IT A TRUSTED PARTNER FOR BUSINESSES SEEKING GROWTH.

CRAFTING NARRATIVES

DIGNITY MARKETING SERVICES EXCELLED IN CREATING IMPACTFUL MARKETING CAMPAIGNS THAT RESONATED WITH AUDIENCES. JAWEED'S EXPERTISE IN CONSUMER PSYCHOLOGY ENABLED BRANDS TO BUILD MEANINGFUL CONNECTIONS WITH THEIR CUSTOMERS.

DRIVING GROWTH

THE AGENCY'S INNOVATIVE APPROACH TO MARKETING HELPED BUSINESSES OF ALL SIZES ACHIEVE THEIR GROWTH OBJECTIVES. FROM SOCIAL MEDIA STRATEGIES TO CONTENT CREATION, DIGNITY MARKETING SERVICES PROVIDED COMPREHENSIVE SOLUTIONS FOR BRAND SUCCESS.

CHAPTER 8 DIGNITY DIAGNOSTIC

DIGNITY DIAGNOSTIC STANDS AS A TESTAMENT TO JAWEED YAMAANI'S COMMITMENT TO TRANSFORMING HEALTHCARE ACCESSIBILITY. FOCUSED ON AFFORDABILITY, TRUST, AND CONVENIENCE, THIS VENTURE EPITOMIZES HIS MISSION TO EMPOWER COMMUNITIES BY MAKING HEALTH DIAGNOSTICS ACCESSIBLE TO EVERYONE, REGARDLESS OF FINANCIAL CONSTRAINTS OR GEOGRAPHICAL BARRIERS.

AFFORDABLE, RELIABLE HEALTHCARE

AT THE HEART OF DIGNITY DIAGNOSTIC IS THE DRIVE TO OFFER LAB TESTS AT PRICES 50-60% LOWER THAN MARKET RATES. THIS AFFORDABILITY ENSURES THAT ESSENTIAL DIAGNOSTICS, SUCH AS BLOOD TESTS, FULL-BODY CHECKUPS, AND PREVENTIVE SCREENINGS, ARE WITHIN REACH FOR EVERY INDIVIDUAL.

BY ADDRESSING THE FINANCIAL CHALLENGES OFTEN ASSOCIATED WITH HEALTHCARE, DIGNITY DIAGNOSTIC HAS BECOME A LIFELINE FOR COUNTLESS FAMILIES SEEKING QUALITY MEDICAL SERVICES.

CONVENIENCE AT YOUR DOORSTEP

EMPOWERING PREVENTIVE HEALTHCARE

THE VENTURE EMPHASIZES THE IMPORTANCE OF PREVENTIVE HEALTH CHECKUPS, ENCOURAGING INDIVIDUALS TO PROACTIVELY MONITOR THEIR WELL-BEING. BY OFFERING COMPREHENSIVE PACKAGES AT DISCOUNTED RATES, DIGNITY DIAGNOSTIC INSPIRES A CULTURE OF HEALTH AWARENESS AND EARLY INTERVENTION.

BREAKING BARRIERS

DIGNITY DIAGNOSTIC REMOVED THE BARRIERS TO HEALTHCARE ACCESS BY OFFERING AFFORDABLE AND CONVENIENT SERVICES. JAWEED'S COMMITMENT TO HEALTH EQUITY ENSURED THAT EVERYONE, REGARDLESS OF THEIR BACKGROUND, COULD ACCESS THE CARE THEY NEEDED.

PREVENTATIVE CARE

THE PLATFORM EMPHASIZED THE IMPORTANCE OF PREVENTATIVE CARE, OFFERING A RANGE OF SERVICES DESIGNED TO DETECT AND ADDRESS HEALTH ISSUES EARLY. JAWEED'S HOLISTIC APPROACH TO HEALTHCARE CONTRIBUTED TO IMPROVED HEALTH OUTCOMES AND QUALITY OF LIFE FOR MANY.

CHAPTER 9: DIGNITYREFERRAL

JAWEED KNEW THE POWER OF NETWORKS AND COLLABORATION, WHICH LED TO THE CREATION OF DIGNITY REFERRAL. THIS PLATFORM ENCOURAGED USERS TO SHARE JOB AND BUSINESS REFERRALS, CREATING A TRUSTED ECOSYSTEM OF MUTUAL GROWTH. JAWEED'S FOCUS ON TRUST AND TRANSPARENCY MADE DIGNITY REFERRAL A UNIQUE AND HIGHLY EFFECTIVE MODEL.

FOSTERING COLLABORATION

DIGNITY REFERRAL BUILT A COMMUNITY OF TRUST WHERE USERS COULD SHARE VALUABLE OPPORTUNITIES AND INSIGHTS. JAWEED'S EMPHASIS ON COLLABORATION HELPED CREATE A SUPPORTIVE NETWORK THAT BENEFITED EVERYONE INVOLVED.

ENCOURAGING GROWTH

THE PLATFORM'S REFERRAL SYSTEM ENCOURAGED USERS TO CONTRIBUTE TO EACH OTHER'S SUCCESS. BY FOSTERING A CULTURE OF MUTUAL SUPPORT, DIGNITY REFERRAL HELPED BUSINESSES AND INDIVIDUALS THRIVE TOGETHER.

CHAPTER 10: THE JOURNEY OF LEADERSHIP

JAWEED'S LEADERSHIP STYLE IS DEFINED BY EMPATHY AND INNOVATION. STARTING HIS ENTREPRENEURIAL JOURNEY AT 21, HE FACED COUNTLESS CHALLENGES, FROM SECURING RESOURCES TO GAINING CREDIBILITY IN COMPETITIVE MARKETS. BUT HIS ABILITY TO INSPIRE AND EMPOWER THOSE AROUND HIM TURNED EVERY OBSTACLE INTO AN OPPORTUNITY. HIS INCLUSION IN THE 40 UNDER 40 LIST STANDS AS A TESTAMENT TO HIS EXCEPTIONAL LEADERSHIP.

LEADERSHIP LESSONS

JAWEED'S JOURNEY WAS FILLED WITH OBSTACLES, BUT HIS RESILIENCE AND DETERMINATION SAW HIM THROUGH. HIS ABILITY TO TURN SETBACKS INTO STEPPING STONES WAS A KEY FACTOR IN HIS SUCCESS.

JAWEED'S LEADERSHIP STYLE IS DEFINED BY EMPATHY AND INNOVATION. STARTING HIS ENTREPRENEURIAL JOURNEY AT 21, HE FACED COUNTLESS CHALLENGES, FROM SECURING RESOURCES TO GAINING CREDIBILITY IN COMPETITIVE MARKETS.

BUT HIS ABILITY TO INSPIRE AND EMPOWER THOSE AROUND HIM TURNED EVERY OBSTACLE INTO AN OPPORTUNITY. HIS INCLUSION IN THE 40 UNDER 40 LIST STANDS AS A TESTAMENT TO HIS EXCEPTIONAL LEADERSHIP.

CHAPTER 10: THE JOURNEY OF LEADERSHIP

AT JUST 25, JAWEED YAMAANI HAS ALREADY CREATED A LEGACY THAT MANY ASPIRE TO ACHIEVE IN A LIFETIME. HIS BUSINESSES HAVE TRANSFORMED INDUSTRIES, BUT HIS GREATEST ACHIEVEMENT IS THE LIVES HE HAS TOUCHED AND THE OPPORTUNITIES HE HAS CREATED. JAWEED'S JOURNEY IS FAR FROM OVER. WITH HIS EYES SET ON GLOBAL EXPANSION AND TECHNOLOGICAL INNOVATION, THE FUTURE HOLDS ENDLESS POSSIBILITIES FOR THIS YOUNG VISIONARY.

TRANSFORMING LIVES

Jaweed's impact extends far beyond his business ventures. His work has touched the lives of many, providing opportunities and hope where there was once none.

FUTURE ASPIRATIONS

JAWEED'S PLANS FOR THE FUTURE INCLUDE GLOBAL EXPANSION AND CONTINUED INNOVATION. HIS VISION FOR HIS VENTURES IS EVER-EVOLVING, AIMING TO MAKE A BROADER IMPACT ON A GLOBAL SCALE.

EPILOGUE: A MESSAGE FOR THE NEXT GENERATION

JAWEED'S STORY IS PROOF THAT SUCCESS IS NOT MEASURED BY AGE BUT BY THE IMPACT YOU MAKE. FOR ANYONE WITH A DREAM, HIS ADVICE IS SIMPLE: START NOW, STAY RESILIENT, AND ALWAYS AIM TO UPLIFT OTHERS ALONG THE WAY.

JAWEED'S STORY IS PROOF THAT SUCCESS IS NOT MEASURED BY AGE BUT BY THE IMPACT YOU MAKE. FOR ANYONE WITH A DREAM, HIS ADVICE IS SIMPLE: START NOW, STAY RESILIENT, AND ALWAYS AIM TO UPLIFT OTHERS ALONG THE WAY.

RARE PICS OF
Mr. Asif Rubsamjani &
Mr. Jaweed Yamani

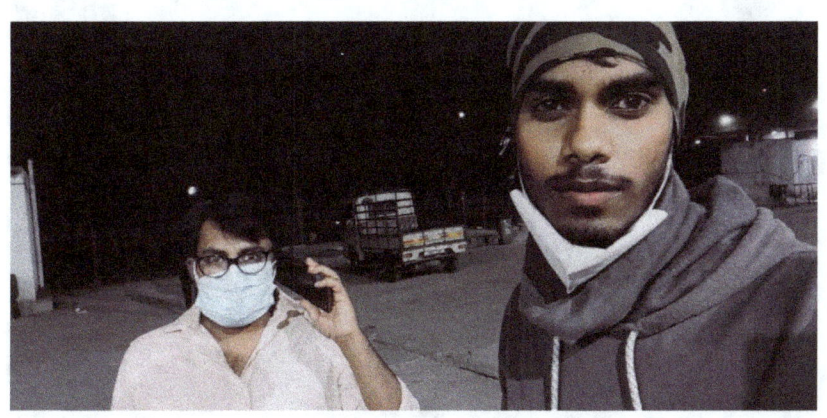

RARE PICS OF Mr. Amer Pasha & Jaweed Yamani

Mr. Jaweed Yamani

Message from Jaweed Yamaani

Never lose two precious things in life:

Opportunities – They knock rarely, so grab them when they do.

Good People – They are treasures that make the journey worthwhile.

It's not easy to find good people, and opportunities don't come often. When they do, hold onto them with gratitude and purpose.

Every day, thank God for what you have, because countless others dream of the blessings you already enjoy.

<u>WRITER</u>
<u>Vikram Kulkarni & Ravi Bhushan</u>

www.ingramcontent.com/pod-product-compliance
Lightning Source LLC
Chambersburg PA
CBHW051534240526
45471CB00020B/2674